WHERE DO LOVERS GO, WHEN LOVE LEAVES?

MANPREET KAUR

Copyright © Manpreet Kaur
All Rights Reserved.

This book has been published with all efforts taken to make the material error-free after the consent of the author. However, the author and the publisher do not assume and hereby disclaim any liability to any party for any loss, damage, or disruption caused by errors or omissions, whether such errors or omissions result from negligence, accident, or any other cause.

While every effort has been made to avoid any mistake or omission, this publication is being sold on the condition and understanding that neither the author nor the publishers or printers would be liable in any manner to any person by reason of any mistake or omission in this publication or for any action taken or omitted to be taken or advice rendered or accepted on the basis of this work. For any defect in printing or binding the publishers will be liable only to replace the defective copy by another copy of this work then available.

Dedicated to my mother and all the beautiful and hardworking
single mothers out there.

Contents

Contents

Contents

Contents

Contents

Contents

Acknowledgements

I gave almost 2 years to this book and finally it's here. First of all, I would like to express my gratitude and thank everyone who helped me complete this book. I would like to thank my parents for standing through every rain and shin, they have always encouraged me to write even when I was on the urge of giving up and they are the ones who have always been a constant support in all shades of my life, my sibling and my friends and each and every one who has never let the fire die inside me and made me believe in myself.. I would love to thank my guardian angel. I would also want to thank my teachers Dr. Shayantani Banerjee Ma'am, Ms. Ayushi Zina Ma'am and Mr. Prabhat Chaurasia Sir for reviewing my book, thank you for the guidance, under you I am being able to come out with the best version of myself especially as a writer. And lastly, I would like to thank all the lovely readers for whom I have penned down all the words.

Kaash kabhi aisa ho jaye

Jo lafz kahu wo ho jaye

Tere baalon ke bare likhu

Ehsaas mujhe ho jaye

Mai zin likhu

Tu zindagi bane meri

Jo pas likhu

Tu aa jaye

Mai ishq likhu

Tujhe ho jaye…

Mere khayal ke dunia mein

Ek aas yahi ho jaye

Mai ye sab likhu ek panne pe

Tu panne ki tarah mujhpe utar jaye

Mai faad dalu jab us panne ko

Tu jod use le aaye

Mai Ran likhu

Tu Vir likhe

Mera Man Preet hojaye

Mai aa likhu tu aajye

Mai ishq likhu tujhe ho jaye…

-Ranvir Sharma

1. ZIPLOCK BAG

this time,

   i am sealing my heart
   in a ziplock bag.
   that way feelings won't seep in.

2. TOXIC UNIVERSE

you began as my universe,
but quickly became the asteroid
that knocked my world out of orbit.

3. NOT OVER YOU

memories are bubbling up again.
of us together,
going to parties and talking all night.
smiling and laughing in the moonlight.
sharing our dreams,
that we wanted so badly to come true.
and again i realize i am not over you.

4. HOSTAGED BY FEARS

deep blue,
all around,
frigid air
stinging my skin.
water pouring
into my lungs.
held hostage
by my fears.

5. ENDINGS ARE BEGINNINGS

heavy limbs
weighing me down.
racing head
never stopping.
unsteady hands
always shaking.
millions of questions
reeling through my head
never ending,
and this is just the beginning.

6. DOLLHOUSE

i am just a doll,
all dressed up in a puffy dress.
with a smile to go along.
i am playing the part
they expect of me,
while hiding my heart desperately.

7. MUNDANE LIFE

it is like a summer breeze,
it is sneaking fresh cookies off your grandma's table as a kid.
it is when you see your favourite artist's art piece at the museum,
it is blasting your favourite song with the windows rolled down
in the middle of summer.
it is reading your favourite book at 2 in the morning with
candles burning in the background.
it is that feeling you get when you are the cause of someone's
smile,
it is drinking your coffee after a productive day.
there are not enough words to describe just how this feels,
but it is a dream come true.

8. SCARS STAYED

perhaps we hurt
each other so
because we knew.
if our love would
end one day,
atleast the scars
we left would stay.

9. MAGIC OF THE FIRSTS

perhaps i get so easily bored
with safe things and routines because
i am in love with the magic of the unknown,
the way it lets you explore the world with the eyes of a child,
every time again for the first time.

10. I AM ALL I AM

i am all i am
and all that i am not
all the loves i remember
all the loves i forgot
i am all that i am
all the things i began
and all the things that i stopped.

11. IMPERMANENCE

and at last, nothing will last.
not the happy moments, not the sad ones,
not the joy, the grief, the disappointments,
the anger, the anticipation, the desire,
the success, the envy,
not the love and not the hatred.
impermanence will always be our only permanence.

12. I AM FINE?

i called you mine
and you called me yours
now you are yours again
and i am fine.

13. NOT FOUND YET

i have always believed that
every thing in this world has feelings.
so whenever i lost, broke something
or whenever i favoured one thing over another,
a doll, a book, a pair of shoes,
i felt so deeply sorry for those that had been rejected
or forgotten,
in these moments,
my dad used to console me with a smile as he said:
dont be sad. they will be found and loved by another.
today, whenever i am sad,
whenever i feel let down by the world,
i remember his words, and smile.

14. SIGNS

i should have known
by the way you held
your cup this morning
(tight grip couldn't hide your tremble)
i should have known by the way your lips
burned silently as if lit by a cold vermillion candle.
i should have known by the way you did not smile
as i spoke about the things i planned for me and you.
i should have known but perhaps, i knew.

15. I DIDN'T KNOW IT WAS OUR LAST

if only that day
i had known,
i would not have left you alone.
i would have held your hand a bit tighter,
and smiled at you a lil brighter.
i would have watched you slowly breathe,
and stayed until you leave.

16. I NEVER REALLY KNEW YOU

maybe in a quiet little coffee shop
maybe in a crowded lively room
one day;
i will hear your name
and i will bite my lip
and holdback knowing bittersweet smile
about a man i used to know.

17. ONLY LOVE

it takes patience for the crescent moon to become full.
it takes wisdom to know the moon is full throughut
but it is only love, that sees beauty in all its phases and absences.

18. DROWNING IN LOVE

falling makes perfect sense,
in your arms,
in love; with you.

19. WHY DID YOU WAKE ME UP?

if the clouds of despair are still above my head
tell me why did you wake me up?
if i cannot perceive my life every day as that of a rising sun
tell me why should i wake up?
if the dreams i am having are way satisfactorily than my reality
what is the concern of opening these eyes?
if the clouds of despair are still above my head...

20. ARE YOU COURAGEOUS ENOUGH?

falling in love takes courage.
you cannot be afraid,
neither of heights nor depths.
the free fall might be breath-taking,
but you never know if you survive the landing.

21. IN THE BLURRY HAZE

sometimes i feel like
an unfocused instant film photograph.

22. TEARS FOR MY OWN SELF

i realized i grew up
when the tears i shed
were meant for me
and not for you.

23. EAGER FOR ANSWERS

cotton candy skies and rain drops in disguise
you colour me softly and thoroughly
mapping me out like i am your whole sea
like i am cosmic dust, waiting to give you all the answers.

24. EVENING WITH ME AND MY MIND

clothes on the floor
coffee on the table
you can crawl up inside my mind
and try to stay a while
but you might be uncomfortable in there
so maybe just sit next to me instead
and we can watch the light moving
on the walls here
and that might be a pleasantway to spend an evening.

25. HOW DO YOU EXPLAIN?

how do you explain to someone that you are drowning?
that just when you have pulled your head above water
and you take a deep breath
another wave comes crashing into you
sending your heart, your mind, your soul back underwater
so deep that even light cannot reach.

26. COME, FILL THE VOID

and so i sit here
drunk on the thought
that only love
can fill my empty bones.

27. I MISS YOU

it gets easier with each passing day
Me without you
Is still such a novelty
Some days
Sadness overwhelms me
Yet, i try to keep going
Okay on the outside
Until i think of you again.
i miss you.

28. WHAT HAPPENS TO BROKEN DREAMS?

sometimes i wonder what happens to the broken dreams
do they melt in the heat like honey
or are they picked up by the winds
and blown away like dust
do they join other dreams
and come together like water
or do they just slowly disappear
like paper decomposing
and become one with the earth
do they explode into nothingness
like a star that has reached its limit
or are they filed away
still ready for a chance to be fulfilled?

29. PERCEPTION OF PERFECTION

minus fifteen

tone legs

slim waist

perfect.

long hair

blue eyes

slim nose

perfect.

oh how wrong was i

any weight

any height

any body

anybody

everbody

perfect.

30. GREYS INTO RAINBOWS

deprived. we all are.
are not we all just divested for something our heart yearned for a
long time and nonetheless still does,
that something which chases our soul but is tamed,
that something which gives life to our dead passions,
which turns all our greys into a rainbow,
that which makes the flower bloom on graves you never knew
you had been to,
but do not we all repent every night because everything else is
just futile
the dearth of some things is unfortunately bartered with our
souls.
and our heart dies in yearning for something we are sure does
not exist anymore.

31. STARVING FOR
LOVE

we all went wrong for wanting
to be loved a little more.

32. PEOPLE

people can never be defined by one thing we are,
by definition a multitude of things
a synchronized machine
full of millions of little parts
working and interacting
so why are we characterized by one trait
one determining factor
when we are so much more than that
she has too big a heart
he relies on his intelligence too much
why do we let one thing
one part of ourselves
be who we are
as a whole?

33. ONLY IF

only if we loved
the way we want to be loved.
the world would be
a little less entropic.
a little less disordered.
a little less chaotic.

34. WHEN I SAW MYSELF

on my back
eyes closed
mind finally silent
i saw her
my self
in shades of purple
beautiful
bold
and strong.

35. THINGS WE DO FOR LOVE

killing the larger parts of ourselves
to let the tinniest of theirs breathe.
-things we do for love.

36. STARS ARE JUST LIKE PEOPLE

i think people
are a lot like stars
some burn longer
some burn brighter
some join with other stars
to reach their full potential
some are part of a group
that make something beautiful
i think stars are remarkable
just like people.

37. DIFFERENT REASONS

funny, is not it?
how both of us,
keep searching for reasons,
you; to let go
me; to hold on.

38. I SAW IT IN HIS EYES

believe me,

when i say

that he loved me

i saw it in his eyes

i knew it when he smiled

it was not just a mere attraction

it was love,

but was less

i saw him suffering,

trying to love me

and one night

he gave up on me

abused me,

taunted me,

but his voice cracked

while saying all that

and in that moment

i knew he loved me

but not just right.

39. SAY?

did i care too much?
or did you not at all?

40. DRUNK ON POETRY

night after night
i sit here
with my pen
pressed against the paper
drawing thoughts,
forming words to feelings,
i did not know belonged to me.
forging my name under seemingly
foriegn experiences.
the release it gives me is so addicting.
a high i can't come down from.
i think, i might be drunk on poetry.

41. STRANGERS TO WORLD

we began as strangers,
just two souls on separate paths.
then one day our paths intertwined
and we became each other's worlds.

42. POEM WITH NO RHYME

maybe we had to get part,
maybe you were never mine.
maybe it was part of our destiny,
maybe our poems weren't meant to rhyme.

43. SONGS ABOUT YOU

and suddenly all the sad songs are about you.
with each lyric cutting into the wounds etched by you.
and every note breathing you into me.
i sigh in between the pauses to feel alive,
to heave my soul from the guilt of you..
maybe that's why i keep the songs on loop.

44. OUR LOVE

our love,
deep,
like the depth of your favourite blue ocean,
like the depth of your blue eyes.

45. TWICE, MY LOVE

and i died twice.
the day i fell for you.
and the day you said you fell for her.

46. AESTHETIC LOVE STORY

what is the worst but yet the most aesthetic way to describe a love story?

compare it to the autumn.

people find it beautiful, even when everything is dying.

47. WE RAN AWAY

we ran away from our mistakes.
now i realise why you were running away from me.

48. LONGING FOR LOVE

i long for a love.
a love in which we can dance
to the rhythm of serenity.

49. WOUNDS STILL BLEED

they say, that time heals.
but it's been a long long time since i got my heart broken
and my wounds you know?
they still bleed.

50. NEVER ENDING THIRST

-would you like to have your true love's kiss for one last time?

-no

-why?

-would you give a thirsty traveler just a drop of water and then walk away?

51. GO, TRY

go make magic in people's lives
because someone made magic in yours.
go love someone as sweet as you can
because someone loved you before.
go lend a generous hand
because someone gave you a little more.
go be kind to a downtrodden soul
because someone stitched your heart when it was torn.

52. I SIT, I STAND, I MOVE, READY!

i sit serene

i sit quiet

i sit knowing there is more

i sit waiting, ready to want more

i stand tall

i stand still

i stand knowing no direction

i stand turning, ready to move on

i move forward

i move away

i move taking on a path

i move hoping, ready to seek forth.

53. WISH YOU COULD KNOW

wish i could say,
wish you could stay.
wish i could make you feel,
how much you mean to me.

54. DUST ON THINGS, SCAR ON SKIN

just like the wind leaves dust on things,
some people leave strong impact on us.
and in rare cases the dust never goes off the things and the
impact never leaves our skin.

55. SLIPAWAY

sometimes
it feels like you are
alone
deserted
isolated
you may have so many people
that care
but you still feel as though
you could simply
s l i p a w a y
and no one would bat an eye.

56. EVERYTHING IS MISPLACED

misplaced socks knocked under the bed.
misplaced thoughts unsettled in my head.
maybe i should be more appreciative of the progress.
but, i cannot help the way pain projects itself.
whenever i see a picture.
whenever i hear a name.
even as things change, this feeling remains the same.
perhaps the damage has been ingrained.
i try to go against the pain, but like cooked rice,
my heart becomes inflamed.
like cooked rice,
i feel like my presence has been boiled by your rejection
and
left in the sink to drain.

57. A CONCEPT OF LOVE

I like you less but
I love you the same.

58. TOO LATE

we reach for them again
but we find somebody else there.

59. LONGING IS TO SUFFER

but between all of that,
there is undeniable suffering.
nobody will tell you that.

60. PLACID PALETTES OF CLOSURE

they say i smell of rotten promises
of unhindered ignorance
and of shattering relationships;
but there i weep
on the edge of commitments
half of my right: of emails and assignments
half to my left: of friendships and conversations
how i stink of butter and curry and stale coffee residues
my body craving water, wilts down to droughts
my eyes, a swollen threat
my feet, wrinkled to exhaustion
my mind, a flattening sleep;
tell me where they sell time
maybe an hour or two
for the sake of repair
of wounded hearts and loaded minds.
i know the sun shall rise,
but who does not love the nights?
to blissful vistas
unattended flaws

crawling content
and dream skins,
do not they shower a couple of verses
on blank smiles and disrupted hopes?
why does one whine
the crumbing of the moon
when his eyes were shut
when the moon shone crisp?
why shall i be asked then
of unheathered meets
and unconsumed letters;
why shall i be waited
for scandals and tidings
is it not ample to see
i am slowly pouring myself
into placid palettes of closure.

61. ARE YOU CRYING?

"are you crying?"
"no."
but i might just be dying
in this room i built from haunted memories
moments in which we almost spoke to each other
these words that catch between our teeth
and nothing seems to be able to dig them out
i have ended here before
with calloused palms and thinking that i could hold on
that i should
and i think i see it happening again.

62. THEY LOSE, NOT YOU

If you got a pure heart,
there is nothing like losing.

63. SADURDAY

How atrocious can it be for someone
who has come so far in your sadness to be left alone on his own?

64. OUR BATTLES

And those who speak of peace
are silently at war with themselves.

65. SETTLE DOWN

i am not one to settle down on anything
and yet you settle me down
like a magnet to another.

66. NOT EASY

beautiful things never come that easy,
even the sky confronts the rain,
to have the rainbow framed.

67. RIGHT THERE, STILL BREATHING

cappuccino stained breath,
lifes question still left,
but i sit still, breathing.

68. SOMETIMES THE THOUGHTS ARE THIS

i always liked stories of people
seeing, noticing the pain, waiting for more.
and when i cannot sleep
i get caught in the 2 AM thoughts
that i know are not true
but are speaking too loud for me to shut them out
so i sit here in the dark listening to the rain
as it comes steady, steady.
turn on the light and stare at the cupboard
wishing that i might open it up
and still find that old tin that held my stash of dreams
or rather
the things that let me dream
lowered me into the river
to sleep as deep as the dead
and on occassion promise to keep me there.

69. JUST A LITTLE

an element of surprise.
a hint of amusement.
a jolt of wonder.
a rush of excitement.
a dash of romance.
a drop of absinthe.

70. I WISHED FOR A FOREVER

he and i often share various moments of comfortable silence.
today, i asked him to break the silence,
as we watch the setting sun,
he was smoking his last cigarette:
"do you have any regrets?"
comes a quick answer;
"no"
another silence
"i wish we can live forever though"
"i would like that too."
and the sun sets and his cigarette burns out.

71. BUTTERFLIES AND YOU

and i eat butterflies
to replace the ones you killed in me.

72. BEAUTIFULLY MENDED

you can't break what is already broken.
you can't shatter what is already in pieces.
but it can be mended together,
a needle, a thread
a heart, and some love.
take your time.
because my friend let's not forget,
we all are bleeding.

73. INK ON PAPER SPEAKS

words do not speak for me.
what speaks is,
my ink on an empty paper.
i am as quiet as the whisper of the winter winds.
but when i write,
i write to sweep the stars off their feet.
to make a flower bloom in autumn.
i write to make galaxies collide.

74. HUMAN ARE FOOLS

he stares as the line go up and down the monitor.
it was only a matter of time
a tear traces down his pale face,
as he thought of her end.
death standing in the corner is forced to walk away.
smiling it exhales, "huh... humans."

75. WORDS TO LIVE BY

think honestly.
speak truly.
laugh heartily.
love deeply.

76. STRANGER SOUL RESIDES IN ME

there is a soul inside me
who is not surely me
for the burdens she carries
are not the same as mine
she walks on thorns and pebbles
with mountains on her head
barefoot, she returns
when the dusk sings of end
her eyes shine no more
her nose bleeds of angst
her skin sheds to misery
her bones wilt to death
her throat falls to drought
and her tongue hums your name.
there is a soul inside me
whose heart belongs to you
and name, to me
everytime the lights go shut
the name peeps out seeking calm
and the clocks stop ticking

the sun rises, but on the other side
tears fall, yet in your praise
my home becomes a fire
scorching my hopes to ash
my limbs go falling
like a pile of dirty trash
the blood drips a little
after every breath
and the soil calls
for me from beneath
my skies are painted black
and my gardens sing no more
my forehead greets the ground
with utmost colour
i cry of dust and shadows
but my heart does not weep
my flesh is now open
to the corners dark and deep
there has to come a beam
that shatters in my soul
when the nights go blank
and the stars are gone
i write to you of hope
and from you i am reborn
i have almost been gulped
in pieces by the gloom
i have always returned

from thirsts back to bloom
i have sung to you a million
i would sing another time
when half my poems scatter
bring other half in rhyme.

77. STRINGS OF FORTUNE AND MISFORTUNE

i cannot believe my luck that she would smile at me.
i cannot believe my misfortune that she does not belong to me.

78. SINCE THE BEGNNING

all you did was make me starve.
all you did was break my heart.
all you did was let me down.
all you did was tear me apart.
it took me sometime just to realize,
that you were doing it right from the start.

79. ADULTHOOD IS A TRAP

hiding behind the same curtain again and again
and would still laugh so hard when get caught.
oh! how simple was life back then
and stupid us, we couldn't wait to grow up.

80. TEARS TURNING TO WORDS

WORDS? they leave strong impact on me.
LOVE? it never came my way.
HURT? is the gift i receive the most.
INSECURITIES? they are digged deep within me.
SHAME? is what i am tired of feeling.
CONFIDENCE? is what i lack in.
TRUST? is what i no longer believe in.
EMPTINESS? oh it is my childhood.
UGLINESS? is what i am identified by.
TEARS? i have shed rivers of that.

81. GROWING WITH A CHANGE

you say i am changing
but i say i am growing.

82. CONSUMED BY NUMBNESS

i drink and smoke to numb my senses.
i know what will it do to me.
the same thing that you did.
came closer while i was vulnerable..
made me confused at first.
gave me joy in the second.
then left me numb.
and now slowly consuming me everyday.

83. HIS/HER

his chest.
her pillow.
his heartbeat.
her music.
his arms.
her warmth.
her eyes.
his stars.
her gaze.
his universe.
her breath.
his lifeline.

84. ONE SIDED LOVE

you have given up on me long back,
for now i see,
it's just me who is putting all the efforts.
i did not even realize when did it all turn into that sick one-
sided love.

85. SPOTLIGHT ON YOU

they were not the one.

they never were.

do not you see?

it is you.

it has always been you.

it is your life.

how can someone else be in the spotlight?

86. SEARCHING FOR LOVE

for a long time
i know you hide her anklet in the lower drawer.
you know i smoke because he used to smell of cigarettes.
i know you write love poems even if you say you don't believe in
love anymore.
i asked you once and you said
"i want to wake up from this pit of despair;
i want to write love poems until i discover love again."
i am not going to complain as long as you feed me on your secrets
in the quiteness of midnight,
as long as i have a shoulder to cry and get to read your poems.
you know i am beginning to like the smell of your coffee more
than the cigarettes
and how gently you play with the curls of my hair.
i wanted a locker to keep my secrets and you said you're not a
thief,
that you also want to save your secrets
but last night i saw you taking out the anklet from the drawer
and putting it on my ankle.
and now, i am afraid you might stop writing love poems

WHERE DO LOVERS GO, WHEN LOVE LEAVES?

or because...
oh god, i am falling again.

87. WHO AM I WITHOUT HIM?

his kindness breaks these hollow walls,
their steel rusts with every loving word that falls upon them.
he makes me unlearn every nook and cranny of this fort and we
walk on, discovering it together.
and nights when i have to camp in a corner all by myself is when
i fear these guards the most.
i fear all i have built.
i fear not remebering who i am without him.

88. YOU NEED TO BE THE ONE

you have to be...
so foolish to ask her out
so wild with passion to chase her
so incredibly mad to propose to her
so deeply in love to marry her

89. THINK, THOUGHT, THROUGH

90. NOT A THING ANYMORE

they told me
beauty lies in the eyes of beholder
yet i see nothing in the eyes that see me

91. READ SWIFLTY

i am an open book
pages sprawled begging you to read me
and you are an eager fool,
hungry to flip through my pages.

92. PAUSES

and every conversation that we will ever have
may leave you thinking
that i am just some faulty connection
to a person who is not really there
because my words come out half formed
and these pauses could fill centuries.

93. KARMA

things make so much sense now
when i am standing on that same lane.

94. PAIN AND SCARS

causing pain to yourself
won't heal your scars.

95. I HAVE CRIED YOU OCEANS

i see my heart drowning
in the ocean of my tears.

96. YOUR LOVE, MY LOVE

when reality keeps us apart,
you are still in my dream.
when each page of my book searches for that withered rose,
that makes me gleam.
your love is indeed spiritual not physical,
it seems.

97. DON'T QUESTION HER LOYALTY

don't question her loyalty,
she'll cut open her scarred chest
pull out her fragile heart
and serve it to you on a bloody silver platter.
just to prove it beats only for you.

98. BELIEVE

believe so hard that
even the hardest softens.

99. DAMAGE TO SELF

All the damage we thought we could do but buried inside. We ended up doing to ourselves.

100. WORKING TO GET IT NOW

I live my life in a constant dichotomy of
If it's meant to be it will be, and if I want it
Then I must do anything to get it.

101. WE ARE PERFECT

To me,
You hung the moon,
Made the stars collide,
Created everything good on this earth.
To me,
We are boundless,
Infinite,
Flawless.
To me,
We could be us,
For an eternity.
In perfect bliss.
To me,
Everyday is still not enough.
I want to look at the stars,
Cross the seas,
La in the sun.
Drinking it all in,
With you.

102. FLOWERS AND CLARITY

I wanted a mind full of flowers
Coloured petals mixing with the breeze
As I dance barefoot
In the afternoon sun,
Lace curtains rustling
Dust resting on the windowsill,
Suspended in a summer moment
Singing honeyed words
To everything I can't see.

103. WHERE DO LOVERS GO, WHEN LOVE LEAVES?

I stood atop the cliff
Watching the lone surfer drift
In a lull between gold crested waves
The world awakening around me
With the sun rising
If I could reach inside myself
I would
Open my ribs
And let the light soak
Into my emaciated hopes
I don't know if anything can save them now
But at least no one knew
How much I wanted to take
The final step forward.
Because where do lovers go, when love leaves?

104. MEMORY OF US

I was just waiting for someone to see that I needed help.
I don't think it was ever that hard to notice.

105. EMPTY DAYS WITHOUT YOU

I have crumbled into galaxies and here I am before you
Kneeling beside these empty days
Feeling every part of me untouched
By your hands.

106. FORGOTTEN

Today I am the half forgotten phrase
at the back of your mind
Tomorrow the exact moment you step through a door
And lose every thought upon the threshold
And there is a day coming when I know
I won't be anything at all.

107. LONELY COMFORT

*Is it odd to feel both lonely
and comforted at the same time?*

108. INEXPLICABLE TO MYSELF

You can explain them the torments,
But how tormented it felt
Will always remain inexplicable.

109. SLEEP OVER LIVING

I yearn for a long sleep,
With few dreams and no reality in it.

110. LIFETIME TO DIE

Tell me my heart,
where have you been all this time?
Why are you so worn out,
Did you try fitting yourself in the box called world again?

111. EVER WONDERED WHY?

It is only when you are drowning
You would do anything to move,
But never on the shore.
And such is the feeling,
When love leaves.

112. IS HOPING OKAY?

I want you to be there in the times
When I am not even hoping you'd be.

113. FIGHT YOUR OWN BATTLES

I was just waiting for someone to see that I needed help.
I don't think it was ever that hard to notice.

114. ARE WE MORE THAN THIS?

You and me

Not lovers anymore

But not enemies

You and me

Supposed to last forever and evermore

But now what are we?

You and me

Not lovers anymore

Just strangers with some memories.

115. YOU AND YOUR FEELINGS ARE VALID

No one can discredit how you feel
No matter how big or small
Your feelings are always valid.

116. UNFULFILLING HUNGER

When people have the thirst to crave for appreciation and love,
they'll just drink it from the tiniest of streams

117. SIMPLE AS WILD

Temporary love scars and ice cream stained t-shirt from last night. Love is as simple as wild as it can be.

118. UMBRELLA OF CARE

I know when it will be raining outdoors and everyone will be inside.
You'll be the only one who rushes over to get an umbrella for me.

119. GODOT

And our heart dies in yearning for
Something we are sure does not exist.

120. TRAGEDY

Apparently the lover of beautiful flowers,
Will never have beautiful hands.

121. I WANT TO KNOW YOU

You were just seen but never truly known,
and all I'll be left here is with daydreams and pretty words.

122. GIFT OF GRIEF

Tell me, my love, which day was it when I went wrong at loving
you?
Was it when you concealed my flaws?
Tell me, my love, how you came to have the knife inside of you.
and let it hurt silently at the same time
Tell me, my love, why did you choose to endure and pick up
every pieces of hurt and studded it to the tiara of love which I
threw back at you?
Tell me, my love, why did you choose to smile
lovingly at me, as if i were your stubborn child?
Now I understand, my love, why you mysteriously departed one
day...
This time, I'd want to choose you.
This time, I want to adore you.
Not to just tell you but actually love you with everything I have.
Until then, I would embellish the gift of grief, my love, in the
hope of your return.

123. WHOM DID I FOOL?

Feeding myself with aesthetic deceit
Dressing myself with latest fashion of distrust
And showcasing you and the rest of the world this lovely façade.
Who was I fooling all these time?
Is it better to be a part of the world or to be a part of myself?

124. HAILSTORM OF DISLOYALTY

You knew it all from the very start,
the disloyalty that I've been showering you with
like it's a never ending thunderstorm.

125. THE PAIN I CAUSED YOU

I see your pictures,
Achieving great heights with a fake smile
But still sunken eyes from last night.

126. I AM SORRY

Every moment you put your faith in me,
loved me,
I merely tried to be a little gentler with you while I ripped you
apart.